$30,000
K

HOW TO LEARN
SWIMMING IN 30 DAYS

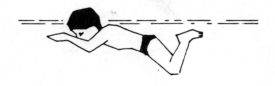

HOW TO LEARN
SWIMMING IN 30 DAYS

Douglas J David
Meenakshi Mathur

 **UBSPD**
UBS Publishers' Distributors Pvt. Ltd.
New Delhi • Bangalore • Chennai
Kolkata • Patna

HOW TO LEARN
SWIMMING IN 30 DAYS

UBS Publishers' Distributors Pvt. Ltd.

5 Ansari Road, **New Delhi**-110 002
Phones: 011-23273601, 23266646 • Fax: 23276593, 23274261
E-mail: ubspd@ubspd.com

10 First Main Road, Gandhi Nagar, **Bangalore**-560 009
Phones: 080-2253903, 2263901, 2263902 • Fax: 2263904
E-mail: ubspdbng@eth.net

60, Nelson Manickam, Aminjikarai, **Chennai**-600 029
Phones: 044-23746222, 23746251-2 • Fax: 23746287
E-mail: ubspd@che.ubspd.com

8/1-B, Chowringhee Lane, **Kolkata**-700 016
Phones: 033-22521821, 22522910, 22529473 • Fax: 22523027
E-mail: ubspdcal@cal.vsnl.net.in

5 A, Rajendra Nagar, **Patna**-800 016
Phones: 0612-2672856, 2673973, 2686170 • Fax: 2686169
E-mail: ubspdpat1@sancharnet.in

Distributors for Western India:
M/s Preface Books
Unit No. 223 (2nd floor), Cama Industrial Estate,
Sun Mill Compound, Lower Parel (W), **Mumbai**-400 013
Phone: 022-24988054 • Telefax: 022-24988048
E-mail: Preface@prefacebooks.com

Visit us at www.ubspd.com & www.gobookshopping.com

© Douglas J David & Meenakshi Mathur

Reprint 2003

Lasertypest and Printed at Rajkamal Electric Press
B 35/9 G T Karnal Road, Delhi 110 033

CONTENTS

CONTENTS

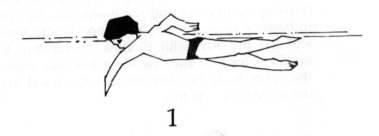

1

AN INTRODUCTION TO SWIMMING

---

1 This book is written primarily with the intention of introducing people to the wonderful art of moving through water, commonly known as swimming.

2 Swimming, an age old sport, has over the years taken its present form. Swimmers from all parts of the world compete with each other for various honours.

3 As swimming coaches we have trained hundreds of people, about 400 to 500 a year, but there are millions of people who do not know how to swim and who would like to learn. Through this book we aim to reach all those prospective swimmers.

4 We have tried to keep this book as non-technical as possible—easily understood and adaptable. It is also a good source for parents who know how to swim but cannot teach their children.

5 The learning schedule is based on a systematic learning procedure to help people to learn for non-competitive purposes.

6 Due to various reasons people neglect their bodies causing the muscles and the immunization system to become weak. But it's never too late to exercise and get the adrenalin to flow. Swimming is an excellent form of exercise for it not only exercises the entire body but also soothes the mind and at the same time it is fun.

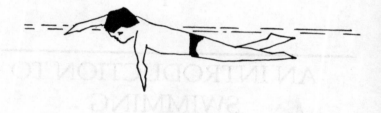

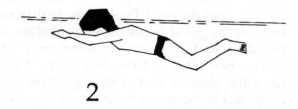

2

POOL HYGIENE AND SAFETY

If not used correctly, a swimming pool can become a
dangerous place. It is essential to observe the safety
regulations.

1. Pool Staff

Become acquainted with the pool staff who will keep an
eye on you while you are in the pool. Maintain friendly
relations with them, for you never know when you may
need them. A disgruntled staff member could take just that
fraction of a second longer to react to your call for help
which could be dangerous.

2. Movement Around the Pool

All movements around the pool should be at a walking pace. The pool side tends to get wet and slippery and can be a cause for accidents. If you do not know how to swim do not walk by the edge of the pool especially in the deep area. You may lose your balance or if there is a sudden distraction you could fall into the pool.

3. Pool Depths

On your first visit to a pool you should always check out the layout of the pool. Pools come in different shapes, sizes and depths. Some pools have the shallow end on one side and deep end on the other, some pools have the shallow end on two sides and the deep in the middle. Some pools have the shallow end with a gradual slope towards the deep and some pools have the shallow end with a steep slope towards the deep.

4. Long Nails and Jewellery

When learning how to swim one does not have full control of one's movement in the water. It is advisable to keep short nails and avoid wearing jewellery in the pool. A lot of accidents have been known to take place resulting in injury. Always try to avoid another swimmer's face—there are many incidents where people's eyeballs have been scratched due to long nails or rings, or ear lobes have been torn when accidently a finger gets caught in the ear-rings.

5. Eating in the Pool

This should be avoided. Chewing gum or sweets could easily get washed to the back of the throat and get stuck leading to a spurt of coughing, water swallowing and may be a panic situation.

6. Eating before a Swim

Avoid eating a meal at least two hours before a swim. A full stomach could lead to nausea due to exertion while swimming, or more seriously cause stomach cramps which at times prove fatal.

7. Spectacles

If you have weak eyesight and are not comfortable without glasses, you should wear them, but tie them up with an elastic band so that they do not slip off. These bands are available with most opticians and are not very expensive. Swimming glasses should be used only for swimming and not for diving as they could slip off and be rendered useless. Most swimmers pull their swimming glasses away from their face to empty out the water that fills in them. This is dangerous because if the glasses slip from your grip they could catapult back into your face causing injury to your eyes.

8. Life Saving Apparatus

It is essential to learn how to use all life saving apparatus so that you are not helpless in case of an emergency. Apart from the safety code most swimming pools also maintain a pool hygiene and personal hygiene code. These codes should be followed strictly, especially now with so many contagious diseases.

9. Noise Level

Try not to make too much noise in the swimming pool. Noise could muffle a genuine call for help. Life guards always react instantly to a sound in a pool just in case somebody is yelling for help, but if there is to too much noise they may not hear a cry for help.

10. Entering and Leaving the Water

Every pool has entry and exit points either in the form of

steps or ladders which tend to get wet and slippery. Be very cautious while entering or leaving the pool.

11.　Life Guards

Life guards are an important part of the swimming pool. In fact it is always advisable to swim only when a life guard is present. You should never swim alone in a pool for there would be no one to help you if the need arises.

12.　Pushing

Pushing someone into the pool seems like fun but can be dangerous or even fatal for a person who does not know how to swim or if he/she bang his/her head against the pool side or pool bottom. There have been instances where a person has become paralysed for life from a fall in the pool. Even if a person pushed in falls flat in an awkward position it can be quite painful.

13.　Costumes

Get into your swimming costumes just before a swim. If you have to swim in the evening after work, do not wear your costume under your clothes in the morning before going to work because it would collect a lot of sweat throughout the day and when you enter the pool in the evening you would be taking the day's sweat with you into the pool.

The pool contains chlorine and other chemicals. Rinse out your costume thoroughly after a swim to free it from chemicals as well as give the costume a longer life.

Similarly people using rubber caps should dry them properly and put powder in them to keep them from getting stuck or spoilt. Do not forget to wash out the powder before the next day's use. Bathing caps are expensive, give them a longer life.

Bathing caps should be worn by men and women with

long hair. This reduces the risk of accidents caused by long hair obstructing vision. It is also hygienic as loose hair does not fall into the pool.

14. Skin Diseases

Most swimming pools ask for a medical certificate before you join up, but if you are suffering from any skin infection or skin disease do not enter the swimming pool for this could aggravate your problem and could also lead to other people getting infected. The water would generally not affect you if you do not have a skin problem but even at the slightest indication of an allergy or reaction consult your doctor.

15. Cuts and Open Wounds

Do not enter the pool if you have a cut or open wound anywhere on the body. Water may cause it to become worse.

16. Athletes Foot

This is caused by bacteria. The skin between the toes and on the bottom of the feet gets white and sodden when wet and scales easily when dry. It also becomes very itchy. To avoid getting athletes foot wash your feet well after a swim and wipe them dry especially between the toes. You can also use foot powder which is available at most chemists. Air out your shoes well and do not wear wet or damp socks.

If you get athletes foot avoid going to the pool till it heals up. Take medication from your doctor to speed up recovery. Always use your own towel and keep a separate foot towel.

17. Oil and Make-up

Do not oil your body before going into the swimming pool. Women should take care to wash away their make-up before entering the pool otherwise it would make the water dirty. It is possible that someone using the pool could be allergic to it.

18. Blowing the Nose

You should blow your nose well before you enter the swimming pool, especially if you have a cold and cough. This would reduce the unpleasantness of doing so in the pool.

19. Showers and Footbaths

Use showers and footbaths to wash away grime and sweat from the body before entering a pool. Footbaths are generally placed or built in around the poolside. Do use them as the walk from the change-room to the pool could dirty your feet.

20. Drying after a Swim

Drying off well after a swim is absolutely necessary especially between the toes, under the arms, and between the legs, because these are places which if allowed to remain damp, could become breeding grounds for bacteria. Hair should also be rubbed dry otherwise you would be prone to catch a cold if you go out into the breeze with wet hair.

21. Menstruation

It is a normal physiological process and is in no way harmful. You can carry on with your normal swimming activities.

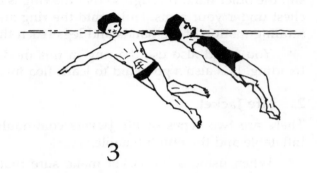

3

LEARNING AND LIFE SAVING AIDS

Learning aids are an important part of any swimming pool, because apart from being learning aids they are life saving devices as well. So you would find these at all swimming pools.

1. Ring

This is found at every swimming pool, and all ships and boats carry them. A good life ring is made of synthetic material or wood. It is not hollow but solid and very strong. There is also the inflatable variety made of rubber or plastic but effective only in swimming pools. As they may be punctured easily, they are unsafe in rivers or the sea. A good ring should be able to take the weight of at least three adults.

In case of an emergency a ring is thrown to you. Hold it at two points and slip it over your head, then slip one hand through as you would when wearing a vest and then slip the other hand through so that the ring is around your chest under your arms. Hold onto the ring and with light sculling motion of the hands and legs reach the side.

You could also use the ring in this mode to practise treading. It is also a good aid to learn floating.

2.   Life Jacket

There are two types of life jackets commonly used—the inflatable and the non-inflatable.

When using a life jacket make sure that it can take your body weight. A life jacket when worn would keep your upper body on the water surface or just near it and with a little sculling for stability and balance you could keep your head above water.

The life jacket can be used to learn treading, or the arm actions as it keeps the upper body near the water surface.

3.   Kick Board

This is a flat board which floats on water and comes in the inflatable and non-inflatable variety.

This is generally used to practise floating, leg action and arm action. When using it to practise floating or leg action it could be held stretched out in front of you. While using the kick board, do not put your body weight on it and do not try to press it down in water as the head could lift causing you to lose balance.

4.   Arm Bands

Generally inflatable, they are worn on both arms. This keeps the upper body—head and shoulders and arms on the water surface.

Arm bands are used to learn to tread water and practising the arm action. Arm bands are useful for children and are not recommended for adults as they cannot take the body weight of adults.

5. Glasses

As covered in the chapter of pool hygiene and pool safety.

6. Ropes

Most pools have ropes, usually with a life tube tied at one end. Just hold the rope with both hands and leave your body relaxed when being pulled in. Do not try to pull on the rope to try and get yourself to the side faster, and do not try to climb the rope.

7. Life Guard

All community and hotel pools have life guards trained to rescue people in trouble. But life guards would be ineffective if you cling onto their neck or pin their arms. It is important that you allow the life guard or swimmer to hold you in such a way that they are capable of swimming with you.

Note

Though periodic check is made on all life-saving and teaching aids, check them before using. The inflatable variety could have a puncture or a faulty valve. If you notice any such leak in them immediately give them to the pool attendant or life guard who would take it out of use until repaired. You could be saving a life.

4

BREATHING

Air is an absolute necessity even when in water. Stress is always laid on proper breathing techniques which enable the swimmer to swim longer distances comfortably.

1. Unilateral Breathing

In this type of breathing the head turns laterally to one side throughout the stroke for inhaling, and exhaling is done in water.

2. Bilateral Breathing

The head turns laterally to both sides alternately and inhalation is done on both sides but exhalation is done under water.

3. Explosive Breathing

Air is inhaled through the mouth in a gulp and exhalation is done in water through the nose/mouth explosively.

4. Trickle Breathing

The air that is inhaled is allowed to trickle out of the nose/mouth. Useful for long distance swimming.

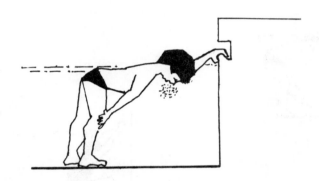

HOW TO PRACTISE BREATHING

Breathing can be practised in the pool as well as outside. Initially a basin of water will do. Start with practising the explosive type of breathing—inhale and then put your face in the water and exhale through your nose/mouth as fast as you can then continue the cycle. Initially give gaps in between two cycles but gradually increase the speed.

Once you have mastered the art of explosive breathing try trickle breathing. Take a deep breath of air and then put your face in the water and exhale slowly through your nose. This is just the opposite of explosive breathing. Exhale fast initially but try to take longer to exhale and keep increasing the time. Next comes the unilateral breathing. Hold the basin with both hands and put your face in the water, tilt your head to one side and inhale then tilt your head back into the water and exhale. Continue this procedure until you can practise the explosive and trickle breathing with the unilateral. Tilt head to one side and return to water to exhale explosively or by trickle. Once you master this practise bilateral breathing where exhalation is under water while inhalation is to the sides alternately. With this also practise explosive or trickle breathing.

Inside the Pool

Initially practise breathing, holding the pool side or ladder. Stand facing the pool side with legs slightly apart and hands holding the pool ladder or overflow wall. Inhale and then bend your knees and submerge and practise the explosive or trickle exhalation. Stand up and inhale and continue the cycle.

For practising unilateral and bilateral breathing stand in waist deep water with your hands behind your back and bend your upper body forward and submerge your shoulders in water. Practise the schedules as you practised in a basin.

5

FLOATING

The ability to stay on or just below the water surface with certain parts of the body above the water line is called floating.

There are two floating positions which are commonly used in swimming. (1) The prone float, (2) The supine float. We will discuss both these floating positions.

It is a fact that females are better floaters than males because of their anatomical characteristics. Children are also good floaters but once they grow older the body weight increases and the bones become heavier reducing the ability to float.

1. The Prone Float

It resembles the lying down position on a bed, flat on your stomach, with hands and legs stretched and the face placed downwards. The only difference is that when floating on water, the position of the legs would be slightly lower than the chest, head and hands. The body should always be relaxed and not rigid.

You will find that you can float better when there is some air in your lungs. This does not mean that you hold your breath for long periods of time. You could just raise your head and breathe and then get back into the correct floating position.

2. The Supine Float or the Back Float

This is just the opposite of the prone float position though the feet remain slightly lower than the rest of the body. This is a favourite floating position and a comfortable recreational stroke with a little bit of sculling of the hands and legs.

3. How to Practise Floating

Practising to float is the easiest part in the process of learning swimming. Most human bodies float naturally but if you happen to be one of those few exceptions don't worry. A couple of days practice is all you need.

The Prone Float: The easiest way to practise the prone float is to hold the pool side wall with both hands (in shoulder deep water). Slide your feet together as far back as possible, tighten your abdomen muscles and bring both feet to the water surface. Stretch your body as much as you can, count slowly upto seven and release the tension in your abdomen muscles and allow your legs to go down. The body position should be—hands stretched holding the wall, head in the water with face down. Shoulders should also be submerged in water and the legs extended back and held together should be about a few centimeters below the water line. Practise for a little while but if you find it difficult to maintain this position with your hands stretched support yourself on the wall with your elbows.

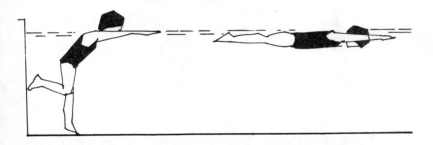

The free glide in the prone position is very easy to learn and once you get the hang of it your stroke learning becomes much easier. To learn the prone glide get to the wall in the shallow end. Stand about 18 inches away from the wall, then bend your left leg and place the foot against the wall and bend your body, hip upwards to lie flat on the water with hands stretched out in front of you, holding a life tube or a kick board lightly. Relax your body, take a deep breath and kick the wall with your left foot pushing your body forward. Move your right leg to join your left leg stretched out behind you. With the thrust of the left foot, your body will move forward through the water. Streamline your body in such a way that your body creates the least drag possible.

Regaining feet from the prone glide position is the next exercise. The kick-board or the life tube in your hand will be of help initially. The easiest way to regain your feet is by pulling the kick-board towards your chest. Simultaneously pull your feet towards your hips allowing your knees to go down and up towards your chest. This makes your head break surface, and you can straighten out your legs and stand.

Remember that at this stage you have to keep your eyes open all the time for sometimes your body may roll along the lateral axis and when you straighten out your legs you may not find the floor. The probability of this happening is more when you are not using a kick-board or float. After practising with the float start practising without it but keep in mind that straightening of the feet should be done slowly

otherwise you could lose your balance. Next try to glide at various levels of water and at various angles also.

The Supine Float: Practising the suppine float is not a very pleasant experience on day one. We would suggest you practise the suppine float at a later stage of your training process i.e. when you are swimming the full stroke.

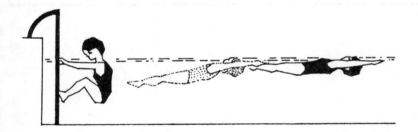

Stand at the side of the pool, hold the wall with both hands, lift your feet off the pool floor and place them against the wall in such a spot that both your knees are bent and are just below your elbows. Bring your body closer to the wall, tilt your head back and with both feet push yourself off the wall. Release both hands and straighten out your body. Rest both hands on the water at the sides of your hips, palm downwards and glide along the surface of the water.

Regaining your feet is easier from this position. Start with lifting your head and chest out of the water, at the same time pull your hips backwards (in the same direction of the glide) and downwards and then place both feet on the pool floor and stand up slowly. The legs should be at right angles to the knees which should be at a right angle to the body. See illustration.

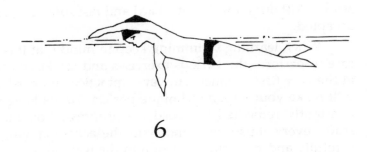

6

STROKE TECHNIQUES

Once you have gained proficiency and confidence in floating and recovery, it is time to learn various strokes.

Competitive swimming consists of four different strokes, namely the 'Front-Crawl' also known as the Freestyle, 'Back-crawl' also knownas Back stroke, the 'Breaststroke' and the 'Butterfly stroke'.

Which should be the starting stroke for a learner. There is no written law as to which stroke must be learnt first. But certainly the 'Butterfly stroke', which is the most difficult stroke, must not be the starting one. On the other hand the 'Back-crawl' may be rather frightening for a beginner as water can wash over the face and enter the mouth and nose.

Therefore, the choice is between the front-crawl and the breast stroke. Being in the swimming teaching profession, I would suggest that children should start off with the front-crawl. People upto the age of 45 can start off with the front-crawl and people above 45 years of age and those who are over weight should start off with the breast stroke. Although this is not a hard and fast rule, it is widely accepted.

When learning swimming keep in mind that it is very rare to perform the various exercises and strokes correctly at the very first instance. However, practice and hard work will make your stroke technique perfect. Faults have to be constantly remedied to speed up progress. You have to study every illustration and read the accompanying text carefully and perform the action to the technique.

To make things easier in this chapter of 'Stroke Technique', we have methodically explained each stroke with illustrations separately, which consists of subheadings such as:

(a) Body Position   (d) Breathing
(b) Leg Action   (e) Coordination
(c) Arm Action   (f) Fault Corrections

Before getting into the actual strokes we would like to give you a brief on the various sub-headings.

(a) Body Position

The body position of the swimmer varies according to the stroke being performed. For example, the Butterfly movement is undulating. It is also important to know the actual position of the body that is depth, angle, etc. The main idea of correct body positioning is to create minimum drag and help the movement of limbs.

(b) Leg Action

Each stroke has a different leg action (movement). The main idea is to get maximum possible propulsion from the leg movement, keeping within the framework governing the 'stroke law'. The legs also act as stabilising units.

(c) Arm Action

The arm movements contribute the maximum propulsion in a stroke. Each arm cycle is further divided into two basic phases, (i) Propulsion and (ii) Recovery. To be precise under water propulsion and over water recovery. Although the arm cycle is divided into these two basic phases, the action of the arm stroke is a continuous one. The most important point to be remembered is that the thrust generated by the arm movement must be projected directly backwards as long as possible during the propulsive phase.

(d) Breathing

Breathing is an essential part of swimming, without which a swimmer cannot cover long distances. While breathing a swimmer must remember he has to inhale above water and exhale under water. Exhalation in water is of various types but the two most commonly used are the explosive and trickle (See in the Chapter on Breathing). Whichever method one adopts it is always better to exhale through the nose under water to prevent water from entering the nose.

Inhalation is the quick breath inhaled between stroke cycles. Initially for practise sessions, the best method to adopt is to breathe when required. This method accelerates stroke speed. Holding of the breath is to be completely avoided as it leads to fatigue and breathlessenss.

(e) Coordination

While swimming a stroke it is absolutely necessary that the arm, leg and breathing actions should be in complete co-ordination. These functions must merge suitably so as to give a smooth stroke and not a jerky appearance.

(f) Fault Correction

Sometimes it is difficult to pinpoint a stroke fault, but once you spot the problem, correction is of utmost importance. If not corrected in the initial stages it is likely to form into a habit.

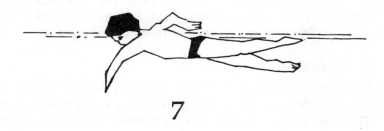

7

THE FRONT CRAWL

The front crawl stroke better known as free style is the fastest of all the swimming strokes. It is a combination of skill, strength and speed which makes the front crawl swimmer such an elegant sight in the water.

1. Body Position

The body position in the front crawl is the same as for floating which you are already familiar with absolutely flat and horizontal, shoulders back and legs barely a few centimetres below the water line. Do not raise the head too high. The water level should be along the hair line. When learning one tends to keep the head too high causing the hips and legs to sink deeper and the unstreamlined body position creates a drag force.

While swimming the front crawl you must encourage a slight body roll laterally which helps the arm and leg movements and also brings the body in a position that makes it easy to tilt your head and inhale comfortably.

To practise the front crawl body position, get into the front crawl floating position. Stretch your arms straight in front of you. The head position should be 'looking ahead' rather than at the pool bottom. Stretch your legs backwards. Now the body will be in one straight line. This is the basic body position from which all other actions start.

2. Arm Action

The arm action plays a very important role in any stroke as it creates the major propulsion force necessary for swimming. The arm cycle consists of two phases. The under water propulsion and over water recovery. The arm action in the front crawl is alternative—while one arm is carrying out the propulsion the other arm is in the state of recovery. We will now deal with propulsion and recovery individually in detail.

Propulsion Phase: The propulsion phase is carried out under water and is divided into (i) Catch, (ii) Pull, (iii) Push.

  (i) Catch—The hand enters the water fully stretched above the head and as it enters the water the 'catch' phase starts. The fingers must be kept together, the hand flat and the wrist slightly flexed, the elbow slightly bent and higher than the rest of the hand. Downward pressure has to be applied on the palm.

  (ii) Pull—Considerable pressure is applied on the arm

and the palm for the pull downward. This pressure determines the stroke speed and efficiency. During the pull, the arm is pulled downwards and backwards in line with the shoulder. The palm must face directly back towards the feet. This ensures maximum propulsion. Learners tend to perform the arm action in a 'snaking manner', which means the arm drifts to the right and left during the pull. This creates a drag force, therefore the pull should be firmly controlled and carried out in one straight sweeping action.

(iii) Push—The phase change over from pull to push takes place at the shoulder plane. The hand faces directly back and is almost straight in line with the forearm, the palm continues to face towards the feet. As the hand reaches the waistline during the push phase it starts moving outward and upwards. The hand is now very close to the hip. The body rolls slightly, to the opposite side (if the right arm is pushing, body roll is to the left side) to facilitate easy lifting of the hand from the water and start the recovery phase of the arm cycle.

Recovery Phase: This phase can be divided into (i) release, (ii) recovery over water, (iii) entry.

(i) Release—After the underwater propulsion is complete, the next phase of the arm action—the

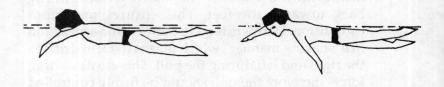

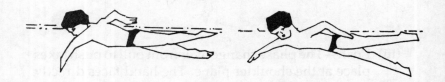

recovery begins. This phase begins with the release of the arm from the water. The elbow is bent and breaks surface first. If your stroke was correct and the push phase was carried out correctly the release of the arm will be somewhat near the hip/upper thigh. While the hand is being lifted from the water during the release phase, it is relatively loose and relaxed, accompanied by a slight body role to the opposite side. The elbow and arm are to be lifted out of the water.

(ii) Recovery Over Water—The elbow must be higher than the hand throughout the recovery phase. Therefore it is of utmost importance to develop shoulder flexibility, because if the shoulder rotation is restricted and the arms are stiff and straight it would prove detrimental to the stroke. The elbow high-hand low swinging action outwards in an arc is essential.

(iii) Entry—The hand makes an entry into the water with finger tips. The arm is then stretched ahead in line with the shoulder plane, the fingers are to be together, hand flat, and the wrist slightly flexed. The elbow is elevated and higher than the hand. Swimmers tend to overreach the entry point, thinking it to be advantageous but it is not so. Therefore you should flex your elbows at entry for this would usually ensure a correct entry point. Make sure that your hand is not crossed over the head, inside the desired entry point for this would decrease your stroke efficiency and create a zig-zag path.

3. Breathing

The main aim of breathing·while swimming is (i) to get more distance, and feel less tired, and (ii) that you do not have to stop your stroke to breathe. Breathing has to be a part of the stroke cycle in such a manner that it does not interfere with the stroke pattern.

There is no hard and fast rule regarding breathing. As breathing is natural and necessary, devise your own combinations.

Generally, during the front crawl the Unilateral (one sided) or Bilateral (both sides) breathing pattern is applied. Within the Unilateral or Bilateral breathing one can choose between the explosive or trickle exhalation technique.

You have to breathe along with the arm recovery on the same side. For example, if you have to inhale on the right side do so at the time of the right arm recovery when the body rolls to the left. The lifting of the right side of the body at this moment would assist the rotation of your head for breathing towards the right side. Remember, for breathing you have to rotate your head and not lift it.

Because of the swimming speed, when the head is turned to the side, a low wave around the head creates what is known as a breathing trough around the face. As soon as your mouth breaks surface you should take a short breath, and as soon as air has been inhaled return face to water as the recovery arm swings towards the entry point. During the exhalation phase when the face is in water, the water level should be at the natural hair line.

Exhalation into the water may be of the trickle or

explosive pattern taking place through the nose and/or mouth. Initially it is best to practise the trickle pattern, by gently exhaling through the nose. This method is also adopted during a slow or medium paced swim.

As long as a slight trickle of air is escaping through the nose water cannot enter the mouth which can be kept closed during the trickle pattern of breathing. The explosive pattern of exhalation is performed simultaneously through the nose and mouth, and the actual breathing out takes place just prior to the face leaving the water for inhalation.

During the learning stages of breathing, swimmers tend to forget exhalation in the water and when the face breaks surface they have to do a double job of first exhaling and then inhaling. In the limited time available it becomes difficult, and generally ends with the swimmer swallowing water or water entering into the nasal passage, resulting in a spurt of coughing and breathlessness.

During the bilateral method of breathing, the swimmer takes a breath on alternate sides at every one and a half arm cycle. The trickle or explosive technique can be used with the bilateral breathing too.

Breath holding is generally discouraged as it leads to breathlessness and fatigue. For learners it is better to practise a regular breathing pattern at every stroke.

4. Leg Action

The leg action in the 'Front-Crawl' is alternate and continuous in the vertical plane while the body is in the horizontal plane. The leg action is important in the front crawl stroke as it maintains the body position.

The leg action can be divided into two phase (i) the downbeat (downward movement of legs) and (ii) the upbeat (the upward movement of legs). But always remember that the front crawl kick originates at the hips, so it is not just

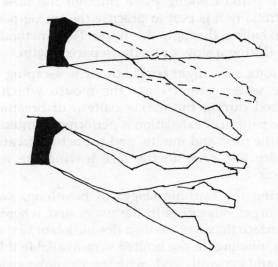

the legs that are involved in the kick. The knees are flexed during the kicking movement.

During the downbeat the knees tend to lead the kick and the toes are pointed backwards. The legs then move swiftly downwards in a vertical plane to create the propelling force. The extended foot acts like a flipper. The legs should not be kept rigid.

During the upbeat the knees are slightly flexed, and there is also a slight contraction of the calf muscles. The feet are flexed and the legs move upwards from the depth of the kick towards the water line to start the downbeat again.

The kick should not be more than 18 inches deep nor should it go more than five centimeters above the water line otherwise it is likely to upset the body balance creating an unnecessary drag. Another point to be kept in mind is that there should be two to six kicks for every arm cycle. This gives the stroke a balancing effect.

5. Coordinatation

When learning a stroke, a beginner generally tends to be very conscious about the various body movements. That is why all actions seem to be disjointed the arms move and the legs don't, when legs move he forgets the breathing action.

The main idea is to let the stroke come naturally initially, give more attention to kicking because if you concentrate on the arms the kicking stops. With practice you will automatically start getting the proper coordination of movements.

The arm action/leg beat ratio should be 1 to 6 that is six leg beats to every arm cycle.

Individual Movements

1. Leg Action
2. Breathing and Leg Action
3. Arm Action
4. Breathing and Arm Action
5. Full Stroke

1. Leg Action

The leg action could be initially practised at the wall. The body is in the horizontal position and the head is above water. Hold the wall with both hands stretched. Lift your feet and bring them parallel to the floor and start kicking alternately feet up and down (when the left foot is on the upbeat the right foot is performing the downbeat). Initially this may be very difficult especially for tall people but with practice it becomes very easy. The depth of the kick should not be more than 18 inches from the water line on the downbeat and not more than five centimeter above the water line on the upbeat.

In case of difficulty of maintaining body position, take

support of the wall with your elbows too. Initially kicking may be slow but with practice it will become fast. Also note that both legs should be together.

2. Leg Action with Breathing

Now that you can maintain the body position and are kicking well, you should also start the front-crawl breathing exercise. While holding the wall and kicking, keep your hands stretched out and slightly apart. Dip your head into the water and exhale through your nose. Once you have expelled all air from your lungs, rotate your head to the right with your mouth and nose breaking surface and coming above the water line. Open your mouth wide and inhale and bring back your head to the starting position of looking down and slightly forward with the hairline in line with the water surface. Continue practising until it becomes a natural movement. The speed of kicking should not become less while breathing. To help the head rotation, lift your right shoulder also slightly. Once you are proficient with right side breathing try the left side breathing. The

only difference would be that you give a slight roll to your left shoulder clockwise. During the last stage alternate every breathing cycle to the left and right side.

3. Arm Action

Practising the arm action is easier. Stand in waist deep water with your legs slightly apart and your hips slightly behind the line of your feet. Bend your upper body (waist upwards) forward and bring it about 2 to 3 cm below water level. Stretch both arms straight in front of you in line with your shoulders. Join your fingers and flatten your palms. Start lowering your right hand into the water all the while pulling backwards towards your thighs. Do not keep your hands rigid. Let there be a bend at the elbow. When your right hand comes near your right thigh it is almost near the water surface. Start lifting your elbow out of the water decreasing the angle between the arm and forearm. Meanwhile, the hand leaves the water, so give it a slight outward swing and bring it towards the point of entry in line with your right shoulder. Similarly you would practise with your left hand. While practising with the right hand keep the left hand in front stretched out in line with the shoulder and vice-versa.

After these individual arm practices try alternate arm practises but be very careful of the timing, when your right hand is ready to enter water, your left arm should start the recovery—leaving the water for the overwater recovery and when the right hand is at the start of the recovery, the left hand is ready to enter water for the underwater propulsion phase of the arm cycle.

4. Arm Action with Breathing

Practising the arm action with breathing is also one way of coordinating your arm action. When your right arm begins its entry into the water and begins its propulsion phase, you should start rolling your body towards the left i.e. left shoulder goes slightly in the water and the right shoulder just about breaks surface. This is the time to rotate your head to the right so that your mouth and nose break surface. Immediately open your mouth and inhale and when your right hand leaves water for the over water recovery the body starts rolling slightly towards the right and the head starts rotating back and you are exhaling through the nose (all the air should be expelled from your lungs before the re-entry of your right hand into the water so that you can start the breathing cycle all over again. Similarly if you feel comfortable breathing on the left side, you should practise that. But you must start the process when the left hand is entering water for the propulsion phase.

5. Coordination of the Full Stroke

This is the trickiest part of the front crawl. The coordination and synchronisation of various parts of the body to form one clean movement to carry you through water calls for a lot of conscious mental application. You could start off in the shallow end near the wall. Place one foot against the wall (as you would do for the push and glide) and then push your body off the wall with your foot and start floating. After floating for 2–3 metres start your kicking movements while both arms are stretched out in front, in line with the shoulders. Start the arm action with the right arm entering water for the underwater propulsion phase. The left hand should remain as it is. Once your right hand is leaving water for the overwater recovery phase, your left hand should start the entry for the underwater propulsion phase. But make sure that your legs do not stop kicking. Continue practising short swims, initially even if you hold your breath and swim it's okay. Slowly with practice and build-up of stamina you could cover longer distances. One point to remember here is that during the complete stroke if your feet stop moving when you start your arm action you should stop swimming, and start all over again. After a few days of practise start the stroke breathing along with the full stroke.

Wherever you feel that a certain part of your stroke is not correct you should practise it thoroughly.

FAULTS AND CORRECTIONS

Fault and Reasons	Effect on the Stroke	Correction
Body Position		
1 Head too high:	1 The chest tends to lift and the legs tend to drop thus increasing the drag and putting more strain on the legs.	1 Near the wall breathing.
(a) Trying to keep the head out of the water continuously for breathing.		2 Practise floating for correct body and head position.
(b) Fear of putting the face into water.		3 Eyes open so that you can see the hairline/water line relationship.
(c) Lifting of head instead of rotating it for breathing.		4 Dip shoulders some more into the water.
2 Head too low:	1 Breathing becomes difficult.	The same points as above except for point number 4, which could be substituted for a slightly deeper kick.
(a) Too high a kick especially at the end of the upbeat the legs go out of the water.	2 Strain on the shoulder especially during recovery.	
3 Snaking: Caused by wide entry and recovery movements.	1 Causes reduction in speed.	1 Try for the correct arm entry i.e. in line with the shoulder— right arm with the right shoulder and the left arm with the left shoulder.
	2 Puts more strain on the arms during the underwater propulsion phase.	

(Contd.)

Fault and Reasons	Effect on the Stroke	Correction
Leg Action		
1 Deep kicking.	1 It causes excessive drag. 2 Extra tiring 3 Causes the body to wobble.	1 Increase the kicking speed. 2 Maintain a shallower downbeat. 3 Practise kicking at the wall.
2 Too high.	1 The upper body i.e. the chest and the head go lower into the water. 2 Lots of splashing. 3 Propulsion is reduced.	1 Lift your chest slightly. 2 Practise kicking at the wall. 3 Increase the depth of the kick slightly.
3 Kicking from the knee downwards.	1 Reduced propulsion because of less propulsive area.	1 Relax the knees and ankles and kick from the hips. 2 Practise kicking at the wall.
4 Rigid kick (without knee bend).	1 Your propulsion is reduced due to backward thrust on the upbeat. 2 Legs being rigid they tire fast.	1 Kick with the knee leading the leg in the down beat. 2 Relaxed kicking from the hips.
Arm Action Entry Phase:		
1 To wide or too narrow entry in relating to the shoulder line.	1 Snaking movement. 2 Change in direction. 3 Change in the natural body roll.	1 Practise arm action while standing in shallow water. 2 If arm action is wide, practise the cross over for some time, and if it is already crossing over practise wide arm entry.

(*Contd.*)

Fault and Reasons	Effect on the Stroke	Correction
		3 Lift head and watch the point of entry and correct it.
2 The entry is over-reaching i.e. too far ahead.	1 Puts the rhythm of the stroke off. 2 Rolling increases. 3 Puts strain on the shoulder.	1 Keep the elbow high-hand low entry position 2 There should be an angle between arm and the forearm.
3 Entry near the face.	1 Reduces propulsion in the pull phase.	1 Practise arm action while standing in shallow water.
4 Vigorous entry or hard entry with flat hand and low elbow.	1 Waste of energy. 2 Creation of turbulent water conditions. 3 Creation of drag.	1 Practise stream-lined and correct entry with the elbow high and hand low method. 2 Slow down and control the over-water recovery. 3 Increase body roll.
Catch Phase: 1 Fingers spread.	1 Loss of propulsion 2 Uncontrolled path during the underwater propulsion pull and push phase.	1 Keep your fingers jointed together. 1 Direct the catch directly backwards towards the feet for maximum propulsion and benefit.
2 Palm directed downwards.	1 Upper body tends to lift and lower body goes down creating drag.	

(Contd.)

Fault and Reasons	Effect on the Stroke	Correction
Pull Phase:		
1 Dropped elbow.	1 Hand generally slides in the water thus reducing propulsion.	1 The elbow should be higher than the hand and this could be practised in shallow water in a standing position.
Recovery Phase:		
1 High hand-low elbow.	1 Hand tends to splash into the water.	1 Practise in shallow water in a standing position.
	2 This would lead to low elbow and high hand underwater also.	
2 Rigid Arm	1 Outward swing of the arm which is difficult to control especially for the point of entry.	1 Practise elbow bending, high elbow-low hand recovery.
	2 Overhead swing of the arm which generally ends in slapping the water.	2 Bend the elbow during the push phase under-water.
	3 Unnecessary tiredness of the muscles.	
Coordination:		
1 Uncoordinated arm action, i.e. one arm stopping while the other arm catches up with it.	1 The stroke motion gets disrupted, you get tired faster.	1 Practise co-ordinated arm action in the shallow.
2 Wrong breathing during the arm cycle.	1 Water swallowing.	1 Practise breathing with arm action.
	2 Tiredness due to lack of oxygen.	

8

THE BACK CRAWL

As the name suggests the Back-crawl popularly known as the Back Stroke is swimming in the supine position (lying on the back). The arm action and the leg action as in the front crawl are alternate and continuous. Breathing is the easiest in this stroke as the nose and mouth are always clear of the water.

There are variations in this stroke which could be adopted too. This would be covered in the chapter on recreative swimming. In fact, the variations in the back crawl, once mastered, are the most relaxing of strokes and a swimmer can swim for hours on end in these stroke positions.

1. Body Position

The body position in the back crawl is horizontal with the head resting on the water, the chest and hips on the water line and legs slightly below the surface.

The position of the head is in line with the body, eyes looking up but a little towards the feet. The head is also tilted towards the chest a bit. Unlike in the front-crawl, the head in the back-crawl is relatively still as it does not have to turn for breathing. The body roll is towards the direction of the arm pulling (propulsion) so as to assist in the backward shoulder rotation. Due to the leg action, the hips also tend to roll a bit and the toes may occasionally be seen breaking the water surface just marginally

The body is stretched to its fullest in the back-crawl. Sometimes, learners tend to let their hips sink which has an adverse effect on the stroke, adding to the drag force and spoiling the streamlined body position.

2. Leg Action

In the back-crawl, the legs kick alternately as in the front crawl and it is a continuous motion in the vertical plane, but due to the hip and body roll the kick is not literally vertical—it tends to twist a bit along with the body roll.

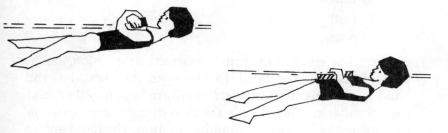

The leg movements originate from the hips. Legs should be close together and stretched straight. The depth of the kick should not be more than 18 inches and feet should not break surface so as not to disturb the body balance and stroke.

The leg action of the back-crawl is the same as that of the front-crawl, but while in the front-crawl, it is the downbeat that creates the major propulsion, in the back-crawl it is the upbeat that gives major propulsion. During the upbeat of the back-crawl leg action, the ankles are stretched, toes pointed, and the knees slightly bent to give that upward whip like movement to the kick. The upbeat finishes at the water surface, with legs straight and toes barely breaking the water surface. As the kicks are alternating while one leg is on the upbeat the other is on the downbeat. The downbeat of the back-crawl kick does not contribute much to the propulsion in the leg action. The legs are more relaxed, ankles are loose and feet remain stretched. The toes pass very close to each other when the legs are kicking up and down alternately.

3. Arm Action

The arms move alternately, just as in the front crawl stroke. The arm action is again divided into two phases (1) under-water propulsion and (2) óverwater recovery.

The propulsion phase: The complete propulsion of the arm action is underwater, and can be subdivided into three phases:

(a) Catch

(b) Pull

(c) Push

Catch: The entry of the arm to start the propulsion 'catch' phase is behind the head, in line with the shoulder, the hand is stretched backwards, fingers are kept together, and the shoulder roll is towards the arm doing the propulsion to assist in the backward shoulder rotation. The hand enters the water with the fingers held together, facing towards the direction of the stroke (hand is like that used in a karate chop) and goes to a depth of not more than nine inches. If the depth is more than that it will spoil the

body position. Less than nine inches depth would not be sufficient for the required stroke efficiency. The wrist is slightly flexed outwards towards the little finger. Pressure has to be applied on the palm so as to start the next phase—Pull.

Pull: The swimmers arm is to be flexed at the elbow and wrist because this definitely assists in the propulsion sweep. The hand while pulling must move downwards and outwards towards the feet. The elbow while initially flexed, gradually bends while pulling. While the pull is at the shoulder plane, the elbow is below the level of the hand, the wrist is flexed and the palm is facing towards the feet. In fact the forearm and upper arm are almost at right angles when it reaches the shoulder plane.

Push: As the arm gets into the last stage of propulsion, it starts straightening with the palm still facing downwards towards the feet for that last bit of push. The hand leads the elbow in this phase. When the arm is pushing downwards it is moving towards the body. At the end of the push phase the arm and the palm give a final thrust the hand is now close to the hips and is straight with the palm facing downwards ready to break surface for the over water recovery.

4. Recovery Phase

In continuation of the last phase in 'Push', the arm when breaking surface in the 'release' is still straight. The arm is close to the hips and lifts out of the water vertically, with the palm either facing downwards, or tilting to either side to allow a thumb first or little finger first recovery. As the arm is released vertically from the water, it continues the vertical movement in the recovery phase also. The palm turns a little outwards so as to enable it to enter the water for the underwater propulsion phase with the little finger first. The point of entry of the hand should be directly in line with the shoulder. The hand should not crash into water but gently cut into it.

5. Breathing

This is the only stroke which presents no breathing problem as the face is clearly out of water. If the stroke is not performed correctly the head may sink lower and a wave may wash over the face and water may enter the nose. But you must maintain a regular breathing pattern instead of holding your breath as long as you can and then exhaling explosively. This causes breathlessness, fatigue and can affect the stroke efficiency and stamina in the long run.

There is no hard and fast rule for breathing in the back-crawl but since the body muscles require oxygen, it is advisable to inhale large quantities of oxygen through the mouth and exhale through the nose.

6. Coordination

Coordination is of utmost importance in this stroke. The body roll with the arm action i.e. when the right arm is on the recovery phase and going towards the entry point, the body rolls towards the opposite side and vice versa. The body should be totally stretched and you should maintain a leg beat of 4–6 for every arm cycle. A breathing rhythm could also be maintained wherein you could set a co-ordindated timing whenever the right arm is on the recovery and the body lifts out of the water you could inhale and when the right arm goes into the underwater propulsion phase you could exhale through your nose.

HOW TO LEARN THE BACK-CRAWL

The back-crawl is relatively easier to learn than the front-crawl stroke. As the face is not in the water psychologically the learner is more at ease.

Initially you will have to learn the supine float and how to regain your feet from this position. This has already been covered in the chapter on floating. Once you are able to float in the supine position and are able to regain your standing position you could start by learning the recreational backstroke.

The arm action here would be conducted fully under water. Place both hands stretched at the side of your thighs, palm downwards. Start pulling your hands towards your shoulders, simultaneously moving your elbows down-wards. Once your hands come in line with your shoulders take them 90° away from the body to a distance of about 12 inches—the palms should be facing the feet. Now start pushing your hands towards the feet and come back to the original position of hands resting at the side of your thighs, palm facing downwards. In a standing position the arm action is something like a bird flapping its wings.

1. Leg Action

The leg action would be as in the backstroke which you could practise individually. The leg action is covered under the back-crawl stroke.

2. Coordination

Get into the supine floating position with hands stretched behind the head. The leg action should be slower than what is normally required. Bring both your arms in an outward swing simultaneously towards your thighs and then do the bend arm action from this cycle onwards. This would be a very slow stroke and calls for no jerky actions. Also note that the legs move slowly and below the water surface. The hip and waist are slightly arched. Once you are comfortable with this stroke you could practise the back-crawl. The only difference would be the arm recovery and arm action (underwater recovery phase) which would be overwater (covered already in the back-crawl stroke) and the body roll.

Now that you have started the alternate arm cycle with overwater recovery, your leg action should also increase in speed and power.

Note: While practising the back-crawl stroke your body should be stretched as much as possible—from finger tips to the tips of your toes. Your head should rest on the water naturally and your hips should be slightly raised.

FAULTS AND CORRECTIONS

Fault	Effect on the Stroke	Correction
Body Position		
1 Hips low	1 Increase in drag. 2 Difficult to maintain body and perform the stroke correctly.	1 Practise the supine push and glide and floating. 2 Place your head slightly backwards and the hips high in the water.
2 Head held too far back.	1 Chances of breathing problems as water washes over the face. 2 Legs tend to lift and break water surface, resulting in loss of propulsion.	1 Lift your head slightly so that your legs drop lower in water. 2 Practise the full stroke with eyes looking at the feet.
3 Body Roll (excessive or less)	1 Affects the body rhythm. 2 Puts pressure on the shoulders.	1 Practise only arm action. 2 Full stroke practice
Leg Action		
1 Feet too high	1 Loss of effective propulsion. 2 Head dips lower or body gets into a sitting position	1 Stretch the body and give emphasis on leg action. 2 Floating with leg action.
2 Bending knees	1 Breaks the body rhythm. 2 Ineffective leg action, splashing is more propulsion is less.	1 Suppine float with leg kicks originating from the hips. 2 Legs stretched from hips to the tips of the toes (practise kicking)

Fault	Effect of the Storke	Correction
3 Shallow kicking	1 Not very effective.	1 Practise deeper kicks while doing the supine floating.
Arrm Action Entry Phase:		
1 Stopping the hand at entry	1 Gives a bobbing movement to the swimmer. 2 Reduces speed. 3 Makes the shoulder sink.	1 Practise the arm movement with legs fixed in the ladder. 2 Full stroke practice with continuous
2 Wide arm entry	1 Reduces the length of the pull thus loss of propulsion. 2 Could also cause snaking.	1 Stretching, rotating and free arm exercises to increase shoulder flexibility. 2 Separate arm action practice. 3 Full stroke practice.
3 Hand entry across the body line.	1 This also causes 'snaking' movement. 2 Elbows may enter water first. 3 Loss of propulsion.	1 Arm action practised individually with a slightly wide entry. 2 No elbow bend. 3 Full stroke practise.
Pull Phase 1 Fingers wide	1 Loss of effective propulsion surface. 2 Swing of hands during pull.	1 Keep fingers closed while doing the recovery and pull.
2 Hands too deep and/or	1 Extra pressure and tensions on the arm and shoulder muscles.	1 Try to maintain a shallow pull. 2 Full stroke practice.

Fault	Effect on the Stork	Correction
	2 Longer time taken for the pull phase.	
	3 Power of the pull reduced.	1 Maintain a deeper arm pull.
3 Hands too shallow.	1 Reduction in propulsion.	
Push Phase		
1 Fast push.	1 Creates more turbulence and less effect.	1 Slow down the push.
		2 Practise only arm action with feet fixed in the ladder or floats.
Recovery		
1 Wide.	1 Drag is created and the rhythm of the stroke is disrupted.	1 Arm practice with feet fixed in the ladder.
		2 Full stroke practice.
		3 Stretching and rotation of shoulders—on land.
Breathing		
1 Head held back.	1 Water may get into the nose which could create a panic situation. ·	1 Head should be held slightly higher.
		2 Inhalation should be through the mouth and exhalation through the nose/mouth.
		3 Practise only arm action and breathing.
Coordination		
1 Body roll.	1 If body roll is not co-ordinated, it could lead to difficulty in stroke rhythm and breathing.	1 If right arm is in recovery, the body should roll to the left side so that right shoulder gets elevated and vice versa.

Fault	Effect on the Storke	Correction
2 Leg beat	1 Affects the stroke rhythm and speed.	1 Legs should beat 4 to 6 times for every arm cycle.
3 Arm action continuity	1 Bobbing action.	1 Practise continuous arm action in the shallow.

9

BREAST STROKE

This is the slowest of all competitive strokes and is the most popular recreational stroke. But as with the other strokes, if not executed correctly it can be tremendously slow and strenuous.

The swimmer's body in this stroke is horizontal (stomach down), and movements of arms and legs are simultaneous, without alternating movements. The head position is such that the water line is at the hairline or forehead. The head must not be fully submerged for that is a stroke disqualification.

This is the only stroke which is done entirely under water i.e. the propulsion, recovery and leg action—one reason why the stroke is slow. Both hands move

simultaneously and both legs also move simultaneously i.e. each limp is a mirror image of the corresponding limb.

The arm movements consist of the hands pushing forward together from chest and then pulling under water back to the chest again. In the leg action, both legs draw in simultaneously under the stomach, feet turned outwards, knees bent, and then kick out hard and wide and join the feet together, fully stretched for the glide.

We shall now discuss the stroke in detail.

1. Body Position

The body position is horizontal, face down mode. The head position is such that the face is looking forward with the water line at the hairline or forehead. If the head is held too high it will affect the body position and if it is too low, the head may submerge in water—a disqualification according to the swimming laws.

For inhaling, lift head just enough for the mouth to emerge from water and inhale. The shoulders are at water level. The arms pull towards the chest, giving a propulsion as well as elevation. This assists the swimmer to inhale as the face lifts out of the water with the minimum strain. At no point do the arms break the water surface.

The leg action is also performed under water and again the legs do not break the water surface. The hips must not bob up and down excessively, a little bit will be unavoidable when drawing the legs in below the abdomen.

2. Leg Action

The breast stroke leg action is simultaneous in nature that is both legs move together and are like mirror images of each other. As in other strokes the leg movement starts at the hips. But excessive movement of the hips only adds to the profile drag and renders the kick ineffective.

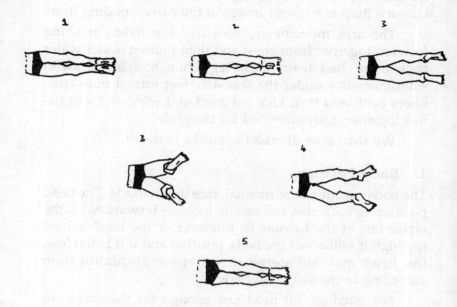

3. Recovery Under Water

We'll start the leg action from the stretched glide position wherein the legs are stretched straight behind the swimmer with knees and feet joined together and toes pointing away from the path of glide.

Start bending the knees and at the same time start pulling them downward and forward, towards the underside of your belly. This movement should be conducted with knees and ankles joined together.

Once the knees are near the abdomen region, start spreading your knees wide that is towards the outside of your hips. When the knees are in this position and your ankles are joined you are ready for the propulsion phase.

4. Propulsion Phase

The propulsion phase starts with the feet flattening out

and then pointing sideways at 90° to the legs and body or line of travel. Then the ankles are separated and brought to the sides at hip width. The legs with feet flat are kicked back slightly wider than the hip width. This straightening out of the legs for the kick should be done with power and speed so as to get maximum propulsion. When the legs are stretched out behind you but are slightly wide, they have to be brought together in a whip like action.

Both the legs travel in the same plane backwards. They are not in a scissor position. The kick should not be too wide or it could create a drag. Another important thing to keep in mind when kicking is that the legs should not kick too low otherwise apart from creating drag it would give the body upward thrust rather than forward thrust.

(a) *Catch:* This phase starts with both arms stretched ahead, palms facing downwards and slightly outwards about six to eight inches underwater. The fingers are kept together throughout the arm cycle. Now start applying pressure on the palm, pressing downwards and slightly outwards. The wrists are to be slightly flexed and must not remain rigid.

(b) *Pull:* During the pull phase the elbows are slightly flexed and elevated above the hands. The wrists are to be further flexed so that the palm is facing backwards, towards the feet.

The hands pull outwards in an arch like movement. Do not make the outwards sweep too wide as it is likely to give you a faulty stroke technique and will hinder your progress and speed.

The arch-like outward movement must be a little outside the shoulder plane. And the last bit of the pull is in an inward and backward direction. The propulsion movement should not exceed beyond the shoulder plane. In other words when the pull has reached the shoulder

line it must stop; going backwards beyond the shoulder
plane is not only the wrong stroke technique but would also
disturb the body position and coordination of the entire
stroke.

When the arch-like movement is approaching the shoulder
line, the hands can start moving inwards below the chin. . .
. . this is the end of the pull phase.

5. Recovery

Recovery is also performed under water. It is very simple
because it means just straightening out the hands.

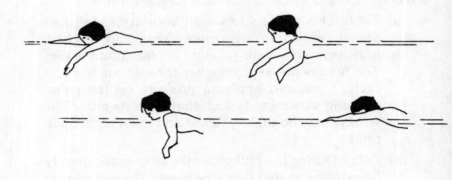

Once the hands have come together under the chin or
shoulder and are pointing inwards they can start stretching
by pushing forward in a straight mode. Both hands are still
close together and at the end of the recovery phase both
hands are stretched forward absolutely straight, with palms
facing downwards. This is the time when the forward glide
takes place.

6. Breathing

As in other strokes, breathing can take place either at every
stroke or alternate stroke.

The propulsion movement of the arms when they are pulling downward and backward elevates the upper part of the body. This assists the face to emerge out of water to inhale. The best time to inhale is at the end of the pull phase, where the arms are the widest and the upper body is elevated to the maximum. Here the chin moves upward and forward and the waterline has to be maintained just below the lower lip now inhale through the mouth.

Once recovery is taking place and the hands are going to the start of the propulsion phase in its cycle, the head is lowered. Once the body is in the glide position at the start of the propulsion exhalation can be done with the mouth/nose.

7. Coordination

Let's start the stroke coordination from the glide position. The body is in a horizontally streamlined face down stretched position. The palms are facing downwards.

Now start the arm action pull. Once the arms reach the shoulder plane towards the end of the pull, the head and chin lift upwards and slightly forward for inhaling. After inhaling while the hands are going forward for the recovery phase, the head is lowered back to the gliding position; that is the water line is near the hair line. At the same time the knees start bending and the legs are brought forward. Now the feet are turning outward and knees are also turned outward, while the hand is about to reach the end of the recovery phase. The legs kick back with power and speed, the feet travelling slightly wide, a little outside the shoulder line. Then they are whipped together and the toes are bent backwards for the glide—this is when exhaling can be done and the cycle starts once again.

HOW TO LEARN THE BREASTSTROKE

Learning the breaststroke is quite simple. You could start with the leg action first.

1. Leg Action

Start your leg action practise near the shallow end in about four and a half to five feet of water. Hold the wall with both hands and slide both your legs on the pool floor as for back as possible together. The upper body should rest in water with shoulders dipped in the water.

Once you are in position, start practising the kick. Pull both your legs simultaneously in with a bend in your knees and with your legs held together. Once the knees come near the abdomen tilt them outwards and then flatten your feet and kick backwards and outwards i.e. the legs kick straight back in the same plane but are spread outwards. Push the legs together and pull them in for the next cycle. Continue practising this.

Once you are performing the kick well at the wall, you could use a kick board to practise. Hold the kick board with both hands lightly, start floating and then start the leg action. Whenever you kick out, you can lift your head to inhale and when you are in the recovery phase you can immerse your head to exhale. Use the explosive type of inhaling and exhaling.

2. Arm Action

The breaststroke arm action can be practised in the shallow end. Stand with your feet apart in waist-deep water. Bend your upper body forward so that your shoulders are sumberged in water. Stretch both hands in front of you in line with your head, palms facing down. Initially the head and mouth can be kept out for breathing.

Once you are in position you could start practice. Keep your arms stretched out forward with your palms backward facing the feet. Now start the pull slightly outwards and downwards the elbows always be kept above the hands.

Once the hands are in line with the shoulder plane this is also the point where the hands are the widest. Place the palm down and bring both hands together to proceed for the recovery. Let both hands travel to the front of the head in a stretched position about 6-8 inches underwater for recovery and then continue this practise.

3. Arm Action and Breathing

Either place your feet in the ladder or the poolside overflow channel. Do a little bit of sculling to get into position. Once you are in position practise the arm action and breathing. When the hands are in the propulsion stage and just before the hands come in line with the shoulder plane, lift your head and inhale and when hands are going back for recovery, exhale by the trickle method in the water.

4. Coordination

Co-ordination in the breaststroke is lightly difficult for the learner, but practice and rhythm building is all that is required to turn this into your favourite stroke.

Take a push from the wall and glide on the water surface. When you are coming to a stop, you could start with the arm action and then the leg action. Initially you may not require to breathe at every stroke but it is important to lift your head and mouth clear of the water towards the end of the propulsion phase.

Body position should also be taken care of with hand movement executed about 6-8 inches underwater and legs in streamlined glide. Then do the leg action in the same plane.

FAULTS AND CORRECTIONS

Fault	Effect on the Stroke	Correction
Position:		
1 Head high Legs too low	1 Shoulders out of water line.	1 Practise leg action with a tube and also at the wall.
	2 Backward kick of legs lift the upper body higher.	
	3 Creation of drag	
	4 Strain on neck muscles.	
2 Head too low below water surface	1 Disqualification of the stroke.	1 Maintain water line near the hair-line
	2 Leg kick tends to be near water surface or above water. Loss of propulsive forces.	2 Lower legs more into the water.
Arm Action:		
1 Pulling vertically downwards.	1 Body lifts.	1 Practise arm action hand low elbow high method with outward swing.
	2 Loss of propulsive forces.	
2 Stopping the arms at the end of the pull.	1 Breaks the rhythm.	1 Practise continuous arm propulsion and recovery.
	2 Loss of speed	
3 Stretching the pull beyond the shoulder plane.	1 Unnecessary drag created.	1 Practise arm action only.
Leg Action:		
1 Kick too wide (outside shoulder width)	1 Less propulsion created	1 Practise leg action at the wall and then with the tube.
2 Legs too low.	1 As covered in body position.	1 As covered in body position

Fault	Effect on the Stroke	Correction
3 Flat foot during recovery.	1 Creation of drag. 2 Body streamlining disrupted.	1 Practise leg action with ankles planter fixed during recovery
Breathing:		
1 Breathing too early in the pull.	1 Creation of slight drag.	1 Practise arm action and breathing.
2 Breathing too late.	1 Breaks body rhythm. 2 Will lower the legs reduction in effective propulsion from leg action.	1 Practise arm action and breathing.
Coordination		
1 Stopping arm action or leg action.	1 Continuity is broken.	1 Free flowing continuous full stroke practise.

10

THE BUTTERFLY STROKE

This stroke demands a high degree of skill and perfect coordination to get the required stroke movement. Therefore this stroke is considered a difficult stroke especially for a learner. Practice is essential to perfect the stroke. This stroke requires good shoulder flexibility. The arm and leg movements are simultaneous and symmetrical, and not alternating.

1. Body Position

The body position can be described as horizontal but the actual stroke position is undulating because the shoulders and hips rise and fall according to the respective arm and leg action.

Inspite of the undulating body movement, the stroke must be a flowing one rather than jerky. The body fluctuations have to be kept minimal. Unnecessary undulation will create negative forces in the stroke, and give it a jerky appearance.

The head is kept in a normal body position except when air has to be inhaled, for which the head is lifted in front. This has to coincide with the lifting of the shoulder and chest for arm recovery over water.

2. Leg Action

There are two alternatives for the butterfly stroke leg action. One is the butterfly arm stroke with the breaststroke kick, and the second one is the butterfly arm stroke with the dolphin kick.

According to swimming laws both the kicks are permitted but the dolphin kick is much more effective; therefore it is widely adopted especially for competitive swimming. In fact the butterfly stroke is now associated with the dolphin kick and not the breaststroke kick.

The action of the leg movement is very much the same as the front-crawl kick, except that in this leg action both

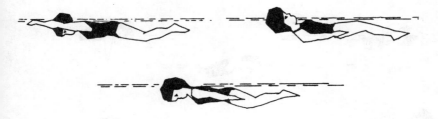

legs kick downwards simultaneously. Due to the strong intensity of the kick, the effect of the downbeat is both propulsive and elevating as it tends to raise the hips.

Usually it is the double dolphin kick that is widely used—that is two dolphin kicks to one arm stroke, the first kick takes place after arm entry into the water in the catch phase and the second kick takes place at the end of the arm pull before the arms recover from the water.

Like the other stroke kicks, even the butterfly dolphin kick originates from the hips. The downbeat starts with knees slightly flexed and at the end it is a whip like action of the lower legs. The upbeat is with knees and ankles stretched, the big toes are close together and turned slightly inwards. The depth of the kick varies from 18 to 24 inches.

3.   Arm Action

Just like the leg action, the arm action too is of the simultaneous and symmetrical pattern. The underwater propulsion phase is divided into:

    (a) Catch

    (b) Pull

    (c) Push

The recovery phase is similarly divided into:

(a) Release

(b) Over water recovery

(c) Entry

4. Under-water Propulsion

Catch: The catch phase starts immediately after the arms enter water. They are in continuation of the elbow-high hand-low entry phase. In the catch phase too, the elbows are elevated above the hands. The fingers are to be kept together. The palms should apply pressure and face backwards towards the feet. The arms start going outward and downward.

Pull: The arms which have been moving the outward and downward direction now change course and pull straight down, parallel to the body. As the arms are passing the shoulder plane they start pulling inwards towards the body. The palms are always facing backwards towards the feet for maximum propulsion.

Push: The hands are pushing backwards, the elbows are still elevated and the forearms and fingers are inclined towards each other. Towards the end of the push phase, the arms push outwards for the final thrust before the arms leave the water to begin the recovery phase over water.

5. Over Water Recovery

Release: After the arms have finished the propulsion, they have to be lifted out of the water for recovery. Elbows are still fixed and elevated in the "release" phase too. The hands lift out of water, not very far from the hips. The release phase can be pretty strenuous as the upper body must lift to assist in the lifting of the arms. Hands are comparatively relaxed, the elbows leave the water first as they are elevated and then the forearms and rest of the hands follow.

Recovery Over Water: After the release of the arms from

water, they are completely clear and have to swing forward to the point of entry, before another propulsion starts. The elbows are still kept relaxed and elevated. Avoid too much bobbing up and down otherwise the body will become jerky and faulty instead of being undulated.

The shoulders have to be kept relaxed and elbows very supple and flexed. The arms swing forward just above the water surface resembling the outstretched wings of a seagull.

The arms now start straightening in front, elbows elevated and arms stretched. The best arm entry would be in line with the shoulders. As the inhalation should have already taken place during the recovery stage, the head along with arms and shoulders become streamlined. Therefore at the entry stage the body is straight before once again starting the propulsion and kicks.

6. Breathing

Breathing is an important feature during the butterfly stroke. Since this stroke demands a high degree of coordination, so does breathing.

When the arm is breaking water during the first stage of recovery release, the arms, shoulders, as well as the upper body lift to assist in this movement. This naturally lifts the head too and offers the best time to inhale (the head is titled slightly upwards). This is a natural movement and does not require any extra effort.

It is not necessary to inhale at every stroke, it can be done at every alternate stroke also. Actually this varies from swimmer to swimmer, depending on the proficiency of the stroke and distance to be covered.

The pattern of exhalation also depends on personal choice. But usually it is the explosive pattern of exhaling that is followed. Exhaling at the push stage of propulsion, just before the arms leave the water for over water recovery.

Note: If you are inhaling at every stroke, use the explosive method of breathing but if breathing at alternate strokes or more, exhalation should be done in the trickle style.

7. Coordination

Coordination is of utmost importance in this stroke and even if a single feature is mistimed or faulty, the stroke is likely to be disjointed and cause considerable strain. In fact it might even be difficult to swim this stroke if it is wrong.

In case of a single leg beat to one arm pull, the downbeat of this simple kick will occur at the time of the arm pull. So the pattern will be—kick along with arm pull breathe during arm recovery over water, followed by the arm entry and the cycle continues.

In case of the double dolphin kick to one arm stroke, generally adopted in competitions, there would be two kicks during one arm propulsion. The coordination would be as follows—the first leg beat is done in the catch movement and pulling of arms. The second leg beat is done when arms are being pushed out of water, over water recovery and entry into water again. Inhalation is also done during recovery of arms over water and exhalation takes place during the propulsion.

HOW TO LEARN THE BUTTERFLY STROKE

1. Leg Action

The leg action of the butterfly stroke should be practised at the wall. Hold the wall with both hands and get into the floating position. Once you are in this position with legs and feet together and ankles facing back, start the downbeat which should be strong and fast. There should be a slight movement of the hip once the downbeat is over. Continue

7. Coordination

HOW TO LEARN THE BUTTERFLY STROKE

1. Leg Action

it into the upbeat but remember not to bend the knees too much or the hip may move more than desired and the legs may spread a little. Concentrate on keeping both the legs together. Keep practising this and increase practice time.

Once you have the kick right, practise the kick along with the tube in a free floating position. This way you would also be able to monitor your kick speed and power.

2. Arm Action

For practising arm action, stand in waist-deep water and bend your upper body forward so as to come in a swimming position. From the forward extended hand elbow high arm position, the palms should be downwards and slightly outwards. Start pulling water outwards and downwards in the beginning then pull straight to the body and as the hands are passing the shoulder plane, start pulling inwards towards the body for the final thrust before recovery. Once you have got the hang of the arm action, you could hook your feet in the ladder or the wall and practise the arm action with breathing.

3. Coordination

Once you have practised the arm and leg actions individually, it is time to co-ordinate the full stroke. Take a push off the wall and glide. Start the arm pull and simultaneously start the dolphin kick. The kick should finish the downbeat and upbeat by the time the hands are at the end of the pull-push phase and are about to be released out of water for recovery. Again the downbeat and upbeat should finish while recovery is finishing so that you are ready to perform the cycle. again.

Breathing is done in the recovery when the shoulders are elevated and exhaling is down while propulsion is taking place under water.

BUTTERFLY FAULTS AND THEIR CORRECTION

Faults	Effect on Stroke	Correction
Body Position:		
1 Body at an angle that is chest high, legs low.	1 Profile drag increases.	1 Chest should be lowered.
	2 Leg movements become slow.	2 Leg action should be practised.
Arm Action		
1 High arm recovery.	1 Slows the stroke.	1 Practise arm action and try to keep hands parallel to the surface.
2 Hard entry.	1 This lifts up the upper body.	1 Keep hand relaxed during the recovery.
		2 Practise arm action.
3 Pulling wide.	1 Propulsive time under water is reduced.	1 Try entry in the shoulder line.
	2 Ineffective propulsion.	2 Try to maintain the pull under the body.
LEG ACTION:		
1 Extra knee bend.	1 The upbeat becomes ineffective and drag is created.	1 Practise kicking at the wall.
		2 Start the kicking motion from the hips.
2 Legs spread wide during downbeat.	1 Lack of propulsion.	1 Practise leg action at the wall and while floating.
	2 Imbalances the body and breaks rhythm.	
3 No whip like action.	1 The upper body is raised and hips are low.	1 Keep hip high and kick with both feet harder.
	2 You will not get full propulsion from the kick.	2 Practise at the wall.
		3 Practise only leg action with floating.

Falut	Effect on Stroke	Correction
Breathing:		
1 Timing.	1 If not timed properly it would force the upper body or head out of water at wrong moments thus affecting the stroke.	1 Breathe (inhale) when the shoulders are at the highest during recovery.
2 Lateral breathing.	1 The body and head have to be lifted higher to breathe.	1 Do not try lateral breathing.

11

TREADING WATER

Treading water can be defined as staying afloat in water in an upright or vertical position with just the head out for breathing. The style is such that the arms and legs move in a pattern to push water down to get an upward thrust to stay afloat. Learning to tread water is not only useful but absolutely necessary as a personal survival technique. It is not strenuous but requires skill and a correct style.

While swimming, a swimmer has to sometimes stop suddenly—may be in deep water because another swimmer is crossing the way and this is when the swimmer can resort to the treading technique to stop for a short while until the way is clear and he/she can continue again.

Similarly treading can also be used in case a swimmer is panicking, and needs to cry for help. Since the head is out of water one can call out. This could happen in a pool or a lake or at the sea shore.

1. Head Position and Breathing

Although the body is in a vertical position, the head has to be held in the normal position as it would be while standing on the ground. But there are possibilities of waves, either in a choppy pool or sea, and these are likely to enter the mouth and obstruct breathing. Therefore it is best to tilt the head slightly back. The pattern of breathing should be as normal as possible, inhale through the mouth, exhale through the mouth/nose.

2. Arm Action

The palms must be slightly cupped and facing downwards rather than on the sides. The hands are bent in a horizontal arc with the elbows bent. The forearm must be in line with the elbow. The hand must perform the sculling movement with the palms constantly pushing the water downwards so as to get an upward thrust to help the swimmer to stay afloat. The sculling movement of the hands is carried out with arms moving sideways with a downward thrust of the palms. The movement must be continuous so as to keep up the momentum.

3. Leg Movement

The leg movements which are most widely adopted in treading water are:

    (a) Pedalling

    (b) Breaststroke Kick.

These are very easy to learn and execute.

    (a) Pedalling—Most people have been on a cycle at some time or the other. The treading pedalling leg

movement is similar to the cycling leg movement. The knees lift up alternately and make round movements downwards with the soles always flat to push water downwards and gain thrust so that the body is pushed up. When the knees are lifted in front, they are at a right angle to the body. This gives the kick enough downward thrust while kicking down. The legs, as in the land cycling make a continuous alternating movement.

When knees are lifted up, the ankles can be flexed and toes pointed downwards (to create minimum drag). But after the knees start the downward motion, the ankle has to be lifted so as to flatten the sole.

(b) Breaststroke Kick—The breaststroke kick movement is performed with both legs moving simultaneously. The ankles are close together when the knees are lifting. The knees move a bit towards the sides of the body unlike in the cycling movement where they are in front of the body. When the legs are lifting, the ankles may be flexed and toes pointed downwards. When the legs start moving downwards, the ankles have to come back to their original position and the kick is to be done with the soles of the feet. The legs kick on the downward phase travel wide (the same position as if a person is standing with legs wide). Once the legs have stretched totally after the downward phase, they have to be brought back together (the same position as a person standing with legs and feet together) and start the same cycle all over again.

HOW TO LEARN TREADING

Treading water should be practised in shoulder-deep water. Stay near the wall for additional safety. While learning one generally tends to stand up very often or quickly grasp the wall in panic. This should be avoided as far as possible. Always remember that eventually when treading water in the pool, there will be no bottom of the pool or the wall to give you any support.

Start your treading practice by holding the wall with both hands. Let us first look at the leg action. Keep your hands stretched so that there is space for leg movements to be carried out without banging them into the wall. Once you feel that your leg action is correct and you are getting a certain amount of lift from them you could leave one hand and practise the sculling movement with it while doing the leg action simultaneously.

Once your hand gets tired change hands and hold the wall with the hand you have been sculling with. Keep changing hands all the while executing the leg action. Once you are good at this it is time to practise sculling with both hands.

You could start off in the usual way with leg action and one arm sculling and then leave the wall and scull with both arms. Initially the movement will be jerky and you may not be able to tread water for long before your feet touch the bottom but with continuous practice you would be able to do it well.

The main aim is to tread water for about five minutes without touching the sides of the wall or the bottom of the pool. This would be enough for a swimming pool but may not be enough as a personal survival technique in a lake or the sea.

Slowly you would be able to tread water and stay afloat with minimum movement. Also try out variants in treading such as treading with only arm actions or only leg actions or legs and one arm action substituting with the other arm and so on.

Points to be Noted

1 In case your face does dip in water, immediately start exhaling so as not to let water enter the air passage. Do not try to hold your breath in panic, maintain a regular breathing pattern to avoid exhaustion.

2 Maintain the body in an upright position. Leaning forward is likely to throw you off balance.

3 Practise in shoulder-deep water only. When you are confident of treading water well then venture into the deep.

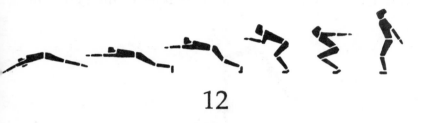

12

30-DAY LEARNING
SCHEDULE

---

1. Day—1

Finally the time has come to enter the water. You must be feeling quite nervous. Don't worry because it is natural to be scared. But before you enter the water keep one thing in mind—you have to read and understand the day's schedule properly and execute the various movements according to the diagrams and illustrations that accompany the theoretical text and you'll be perfectly fine.

Enter the pool at the shallow end (ideal would be a pool where the water level is just a few inches higher than the waist when standing straight). Leave the ladder and wade along the side of the pool with one hand holding the wall, legs slightly apart and bent at the knees so that your shoulders are submerged in water. In case of difficulty you can slide your feet along the bottom of the pool. Keep wading for 15 minutes and also leave the wall and stretch your arms on the water surface with circular motion for balance.

The second exercise for the day is picking objects from the bottom of the pool. Throw an unbreakable and rustproof object e.g. key chains, coins etc. about two feet away from you. Give it time to sink to the bottom of the pool. Put

your head under water and try to pick up the object. The main aim of this exercise is to get used to keeping your eyes open under water. Do not memorize the position of the thrown object and pick it up with your eyes closed. The whole purpose of the exercise would then be defeated. You could practise object picking for about 10 minutes.

Propulsion is very important while swimming through water and kicking is an important propulsive unit. It also acts as a body stabilizing unit which is why so much emphasis is given to learning and executing the proper kicking technique. Hold the side wall with both hands and slide your feet as far behind you as possible. Dip your shoulders in the water, lighten your abdomen muscles, bring your feet to water surface i.e. parellel to the bottom and start kicking. The motion of your legs should be alternate kicking without bending the knees. Keep feet extended while practising kicking. Initially it would seem difficult but with continuous efforts and practise it will become very easy.

You now come to another very important aspect of your training i.e. breathing. Practise breathing and kicking for 30 minutes alternately.

Now that your breathing is synchronized and coming easy in the water and you are able to keep your eyes open while doing this exercise you could try some more picking up of objects from the pool bottom. This time you could throw a coin about five metres away wade upto that point and bend and pick up the coin. Do this for about five minutes and get back to the wall and do some more of kicking to loosen up your body and then leave the pool for the day.

Note: Whenever entering or leaving the pool do not hurry because you may slip on the ladder and get hurt.

2. Day–2

Warm up either at the changing room or at the pool side before entering the pool. Enter the pool in the shallow end and wade in it for a few minutes forward, sidewards and backwards.

Practise your kicking paying attention to the position of the feet and knees. The feet should be extended away from the body and the knees should not be bent too much. After about 10 minutes of vigorous kicking do some breathing exercises with explosive exhaling. This would help the body get more oxygen and help it to relax faster.

You should then do some abdomen exercises but make

sure your body is absolutely parallel to the floor and stretched out. Do 3 sets × 5 sets of 10 seconds each.

It is time to leave the wall and practise floating, i.e. the push and glide and the recovery. You have to be very careful in the beginning. You may use a kick board or tube. Keep practising floating so that you are able to do about 8 to 10 metres before stopping for air.

The last 10 minutes could be kept for practising kicking near the wall.

3. Day–3

Before entering the swimming pool for your training session do some free hand exercises to warm up and also loosen up your calf and thigh muscles. Do some deep breathing exercises, and you are ready to enter the swimming pool. Get in at the shallow end of the pool and get to the wall and practise kicking for about 15 minutes alongwith breathing exercises. After practising the kicking give more stress to the speed and power of your leg stroke.

Get hold of a kick board and practise floating along with breathing and kicking. You could also practise the body roll while floating. After that you could keep the last 10 minutes for picking up objects from the pool floor as you did on your very first day in the pool.

4. Day–4

Start your usual warm up with some free hand exercises, shoulder and hip joint rotations. Enter the pool after this and continue the warm up with about 10 minutes of kicking at the wall. After that you could practise floating along with kicking and breathing for about 15 minutes, using the kick board. The next 30 minutes could be utilised to practise the armaction.

The arm action is very important for any stroke because the maximum propulsion is derived from the arm action.

The other important factor to be kept in mind is what you learn now will become a habit which later on would be difficult to break. It is essential that you perform the arm action correctly giving you necessary distance or speed.

You have to at this stage decide which stroke you are going to learn first. With experience we would suggest that you go in for the front crawl. In case you are overweight you could begin with the breast stroke. Practise the relevant arm action for about 30 minutes with breaks. The last five minutes should be used for practising kicking.

5. Day–5

Warm up as usual especially the shoulders and legs. Enter the pool and practise kicking for about 15 minutes. For 10 minutes practise the arm action away from the wall in waist-deep water. Take a couple of minutes, break and then practise floating using only arms for propulsion. Do not use your feet. While practising this hold your breath with your head in the water and look down and most important keep your eyes open. You should be able to get 7 arm cycles quite easily in just one breath which should make you cover a distance of at least 7 metres. Practise this for 25 minutes and then get back to the wall for more kicking. Your should now keep your legs absolutely parallel to the floor without bending the knees. The power in your kicks should increase along with the speed of kicking.

6. Day–6

It is now time when you can perform the full stroke. Before you get on to the full stroke practice warm up in the pool with 10 minutes of kicking and some deep breathing exercises simultaneously. The most important thing to be kept in mind is that you should remain in the shallow end only and the factors that would help you swim in a straight line are:

(a) You should keep your eyes open so that you know where you are.

(b) Arm action and pull-push motions of both hands should be equal. There are less chances of your travelling off your path.

(c) Both feet should generate equal thrust. . . . and should be used effectively to maintain direction.

7. Day–7

Begin your lessons with kicking for about 10 minutes and practise 'Treading'. Inform the life guard at you would be practising treading in slightly deeper water so that he can keep a watch on you. Treading should be done in shoulder deep water initially with one hand holding the wall. Practise treading for about 30 minutes. Do take two-minute breaks in between whenever tired. Once you finish with treading, practise floating on your back. See back floating in the back-crawl. When the body is slightly relaxed finish off the day's practice with another 10 minutes of treading.

8. Day–8

Begin with kicking as usual for about five minutes to warm up your body. Once you have done that you can do some breathing exercises for about five minutes. Practise both trickle breathing as well as explosive breathing. Get to shoulder-deep water and practise treading for 10 minutes. After that you can get back to waist-deep water and practise the full stroke, for 10 minutes. The next half hour check out your performance.

9. Day–9

Five minutes of kicking should warm up the body nicely. Practise the full stroke for about forty minutes concentrating on individual movements that is the arm action the entry, the catch, the pull, the push and the recovery, the body position wherein the least drag is created, the leg action so that you get maximum propulsion and thrust. Don't forget to concentrate on your breathing which would now start becoming a very important factor as you would now start covering longer distances. Call it a day after 10 minutes of treading and about five minutes of kicking.

10. Day–10

The training starts with kicking for about five minutes and then practising the full stroke for about thirty minutes concentrating on individual movements. Also try synchronizing your movements so that you preform the full stroke with perfect timing and coordination. At this point, speed and distance are not important. What is important is the coordination of movements and also the coordination of breathing. Divide the remaining 25 minutes between treading and kicking.

11. Day–11

Today is the day when you can relax watching others swim. You would also be in a position to compare different styles used by different swimmers and the effect of it on their speed, rhythm and stamina. You would notice some swimmers are sloppy in their actions and they swim across the length or width of the pool laboriously but some swimmers seem to glide in the water effortlessly without splashing much water. This is what you should aim for. Study the timing of the breathing, arm action and leg action, and various swimming styles.

12. Day–12

After the initial 10 minutes kicking, you should start treading water with one hand on the wall and then release it while treading. You may be able to tread water for 15 seconds only—if you feel you are going down, hold the wall. Continue the same movements over and over again with breaks until you reach a stage when you can tread water for about one minute at least. Keep the last 20 minutes for prectising the full stroke. This should still be done in the shallow end of the pool.

Note: Treading should be done next to the wall in shoulder-deep water only. Read the chapter on treading carefully.

13. Day–13

Another day when you give more stress to treading you should be able to do at least two minutes of treading continuously. You should practise treading for about 30 minutes and then start practising the full stroke for about 25 minutes and end the day with five minutes of kicking.

14. Day–14

After your initial five minutes warm-up, start practising the full stroke. Now is the time to start concentrating on speed and power. Until now you were just swimming in water without giving much thought to these. The points to be kept in mind are:

1. Correct body position
2. Correct arm action—which should be faster and more powerful.
3. Correct leg action with a powerful whip back kick in the breaststroke, up and downbeat in the other strokes.
4. Synchronising of breathing with body movements. This is the most important thing to' master.

Also start working on your stamina. You should now be able to do one full width of the pool non-stop and in your one-hour session you should be able to do at least 20 widths with breaks.

You could keep the last five minutes for treading water. This time you can go into slightly deeper water. But make sure you inform the life guard.

15. Day–15

It is time for your second assessment. Keep practising the full stroke for about half-an-hour. You could ask the life guard to check you on the following: treading water, the full stroke stamina, speed. And you could also ask him if your arm action and the leg action are correct. Save the last five minutes for practising treading and then you can pack up for the day.

16. Day–16

Keep practising treading and the full stroke alternately. Speed and stamina should now be concentrated upon. Even while practising treading, you should aim to feel more relaxed doing it and you should be in a position to tread for about three minutes continuously. You should also be in a position to swim about 30 breadths of the pool in your stipulated one hour schedule. The more you practise the full stroke the better it is. But you should keep one thing in mind: you are now at a very crucial stage of learning and whatever you pick up now will form into a habit and would be very difficult to change later. Follow the text and illustrations correctly and your style would become a wonderful sight in the pool.

17. Day–17

Avoid doing the full stroke. What you are required to do is to practise the stroke in break-up actions as you used to practise earlier, that is only the arm action, only kicking, only breathing and breathing and arm action. This time however all actions should be faster and stronger. Treading can be the other part of the day's training schedule.

18. Day–18

Let us now do something different in the pool. We sometimes call it the "Dead man's bluff". This has to be practised strictly in the shallow end where the water is not more than

one metre. Stand in the water with your legs slightly apart and hands above your head. Take a deep breath and just fall forward with your feet still planted on the floor of the pool. Once you are submerged in water completely, start exhaling. You will find your body beginning to sink. Press yourself down to the floor and lie down flat on the floor with your full body touching the floor as long as you can hold your breath, then come up for air and rest for a couple of minutes breathing deeply. Repeat the exercise again. Continue for about 30 minutes including your breaks. Now you can do treading for 10 minutes and the remaining 20 minutes you could spend practising the full stroke.

19. Day–19

Start your training session with 10 minutes of kicking and

then move on to 10 minutes of treading. Once you have practised treading you can start practising the full stroke. This time you can go into slightly deeper water i.e. shoulder-deep but that is only if you are confident of your treading water, and even so you should always tell the life guard to keep an eye on you. The last 10 minutes could be kept to practise treading.

20. Day–20

We will now get back to underwater swimming. Before starting you should do 10 minutes of powerful kicking. Underwater swimming is quite easy. The only problem would now be to keep your body underwater. There has been a noticeable change. Earlier it was difficult to keep the body above water, now, the opposite applies. Practise underwater swimming for about 20 minutes. The balance 30 minutes could be used for practising swimming (full stroke) and treading.

21. Day–21

Now if you are confident, you could start attempting to swim in the deep but make sure the life guard is close by and in a position to reach you fast. You could start with five minutes of kicking, then swim along the wall towards the deep. You should not at any stage panic because this could be dangerous. Keep an open mind, full of confidence. At any stage if you feel you cannot go any more hold on to the wall and if for any reason you cannot get to the wall, don't panic. Just start treading water and move towards the wall slowly. In case you have a friend who is a good swimmer, he or she could accompany you and in case of a problem could just push you towards the wall gently. Another useful survival technique is floating. If you get tired while swimming and feel that you are going down, treading is the best, but if you get tired while treading you should just float on the water with your hands stretched in front, using only the front-crawl alternate kick for propulsion. When you regain strength start using your arms also. Practise the full stroke near the wall going from shallow to deep and back to shallow. But don't overdo it. Take enough rest between lengths. The last 10 minutes could be split up between treading water and kicking.

22. Day–22

By now you should be swimming in deep water. This time you could swim slightly away from the wall but you must tell the life guard to keep an eye on you. Now it is for you to practise as much as you can. This is the time to develop your stamina and style and you must also practise your treading.

23. Day–23

Start with about five minutes of kicking and then start practising the full stroke. This could be done from the shallow end to the deep end close to the wall. Whenever you are in trouble start treading water. Also tell the life guard to keep an eye on you. Always keep in mind: if you feel that you cannot swim anymore or can't tread water anymore and you are going to sink, shout out for help. There are known experiences in the past where swimmers have not shouted for help for fear of being ridiculed. There is no compromise with water. Life is also very precious so feel free to shout for help when in trouble. After practise for 20 minutes you could practise treading. Treading is important because it's your only passport to safety. After treading get to the shallow and practise the push and glide and rolls, and you could also practise underwater swimming. Finish your lesson for the day with one length of full stroke and five minutes of kicking.

24. Day–24

Get into the pool and practise treading for five minutes.

Come to the shallow end of the pool and stand about five metres from the side so that you are not right in the middle or not too close to the side wall of the pool. Start swimming towards the other end of the pool, make sure the other end of the pool is not more than 25 metres away. If that is the case you could swim the width of the pool in water seven feet deep. Do about ten to twelve lengths or widths of the pool with braaks. Rest for a while and practise a little treading and then come back to the shallow and practise on the spot arm action, on the spot breathing along with arm action and kicking.

25. Day–25

Now that you are doing pretty well in swimming, it is time to give more emphasis on stamina and speed. You should start doing more number of lengths and these should be supplemented with treading. You should be able to tread water for at least four minutes continuously. And by now you should be swimming across the deep end. You should also now start practising swimming across the length of the pool with one or two stops in the middle where you tread and then continue swimming.

26. Day–26

Practise kicking for about five minutes and after that get into the full stroke and keep at it with powerful arm and leg actions. The only way to build stamina is by swimming longer distances and using the proper breathing technique. Substitute swimming with floating and underwater swimming. When tired use floats to relax yourself. The last five minutes could be kept for practising kicking.

27. Day–27

Practise the full stroke for about half-an-hour with ample breaks. You should be able to swim well now. The remaining half-an-hour could be spent practising recreational swimming.

28. Day–28

Remain in the shallow for 10 minutes, practising the arm action, breathing and leg action and then go to the deeper end and practise the full stroke. Also practise treading alternately. Do this for about 30 minutes and then do some recreational swimming. Finish your session with five minutes of kicking.

29. Day–29

After about five minutes of treading water and 30 minutes of full stroke swimming practise jumping. This should be done in seven feet of water. The last five minutes could be kept for practising kicking.

30. Day–30

On the last day of the training programme practise jumping and recreational swimming. End your session with 10 minutes of vigorous kicking.

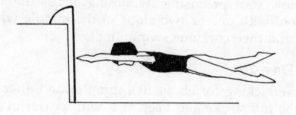

13

UNDERWATER SWIMMING

Underwater swimming is a good fun and also helps the swimmer to have more control over the body and its movements in water.

Underwater swimming is of various types but the two most commonly used strokes are:

1. The Breaststroke
2. The Hybrid Breaststroke.

1. The Breaststroke

It is more or less same as the stroke performed at water surface except that this is performed under water with the total body submerged.

2.   Arm Action

The arm action is the same as in the breaststroke except that now instead of the pull of the hands stopping in line with the shoulder plane, the hands take a wider sweep and travel all the way to the sides of the thighs.

3.   Leg Action

The leg action is the same as the breaststroke leg action.

4.   Breathing

You have to inhale before submerging into the water. Once the body is under water exhale through your nose in the trickle method over the duration of the swim underwater.

5.   Coordination

Coordination is very simple. Inhalation takes place before submerging. Once you are under water the head, arms and waist are slightly lower than the legs. This prevents the propulsion to take the body to the surface. From the hands in the front stretched position, make a wide sweeping arc outwards, till the shoulder pains. The palms are slightly cupped and the wrists are flexed. In the inward sweep the hands whip inside towards the thigh, the legs are stretched behind you. The face is at about 45° angle facing downwards.

The body starts gliding in the water. When you feel the momentum going down start the kick action that is the same as the breaststroke recovery and propulsion. Always the legs are slightly higher than the upper body. Glide some more and then start the arm action. This should gradually become a continuous and faster action. All the while exhale by the trickle method or hold your breath.

6.   Underwater Swimming—Crawl Kick

Underwater swimming with the free style that is the crawl

kick is another variant of the stroke. The body position, breathing and arm action are the same. But the leg action would be the same as in the front crawl kick, so that the body is getting continuous propulsion.

To surface from the underwater stroke lift your head and upper body upward and forward and push your legs lower so that the propulsion of your arms and legs creates a thrust which takes you to the surface.

The most important points to be kept in mind are:

1. Always keep your eyes open under water.
2. Don't wait for the last minute to surface otherwise there is a chance of involuntary inhaling and drinking water.
3. Inhale only after you break surface and the mouth and nose are well out of the water.
4. For covering longer distances and staying longer under water you would have to practise holding your breath.

14

JUMPING AND DIVING

Once you can confidently accross the pool and can tread water well, you are ready for jumping and diving into the pool. It is really a great fun to watch someone executing a perfect jump or dive but believe me greater fun to watch people watching you dive. There is nothing to it except practice, body positioning, and the underwater recovery and glide so that no accidents take place.

We shall now explain the simple jump, in an absolutely vertical position.

Stand at the pool side (at the six feet mark), your toes gripping the edge of the pool. Stand in a vertical upright position, looking straight ahead or slightly upwards. The general tendency of a learner to enter water with hands flapping, makes you lose balance and is painful when the hands slap the water. You could instead use the following

arm positions. Cross your arms over the chest that is the left hand is grasping the right shoulder and the right hand is grasping the left shoulder or you could keep both hands at your sides along your thighs.

Take a deep breath and step forward into the water. Take a big step so that your point of entry is away from the pool side otherwise you may get hurt. Once in the air, keep your body stiff. Keep looking forward and not downward. Bring your body forward in a vertical upright position and join the legs together, gravity takes over and does the rest.

After the feet enter into the water, release the position of your arms and tread water. While entering water you should keep your mouth closed and exhale through the nose continuously otherwise water may enter the nose and mouth and choke you. The normal buoyancy factor of the human body will bring you back to the surface. Keep your eyes open so you know which direction you are facing and which side the pool wall is. Gently start treading water and you could either swim poolwards or swim to the pool side.

Points to Remember

1 Jump away from the pool side or you may get hurt.
2 Keep your body in an upright vertical position.
3 When entering water exhale through the nose by the trickle breathing method.
4 When surfacing keep your eyes open to retain your bearings.

Sitting Dive

Once the fear of jumping into the water is overcome practise more elegant entries into the water by diving. We are covering diving in three stages which would be easy for you to learn and perform.

Initially you would prefer the sitting dive, for this is the simplest form of diving. As you are very near the water surface the chances of getting hurt while diving are the least. In fact this is an ideal practice for the actual plunge dive.

Sit at the edge of the pool with your legs together, resting on the poolside overflow wall. The toes should grip the wall to get a strong foothold. Stretch your arms in front slightly downwards, pointing to the water surface. Tuck your head firmly between your arms and look at your feet.

After positioning yourself start the actual dive by taking a deep breath and raising your hips. Simultaneously your upper body with arms stretched and head tucked between them moves downwards. When you raise your hips your legs start straightening out but before that happens take a push off the wall with your feet.

The entry into water would be with your fingers first, followed by your arms, head and upper body. While making the entry, your body should be totally stretched out with your legs held firmly together and totally straight.

The body should enter water at 45° angle. After the

entry, let the body glide in water until you surface. You could then start stroking or treading.

Points to be Noted

1 Body should be relaxed.

2 Legs should be kept together and head should be tucked between both arms.

3 Take a deep breath (this would also help you surface faster).

4 Entry should be at 45° angle.

5 After the entry, the glide should be with hands stretched in front so that you do not hit your head against the pool floor.

6 Glide should be shallow.

7 At the last minute just before entry, learners always tend to lift their head and chest. This should be avoided as falling in an unstreamlined position is quite painful.

8 This dive should be conducted in at least six feet deep water to cater to error margins.

Kneeling Dive

The kneeling dive is the next step towards the plunge dive. It is easy to practise and execute.

Position yourself on the poolside in the following manner. Stand with your left foot at the pool edge with the toes bent over the side gripping the wall. Take your right foot and bend your knees so that your right knee is at the side of your left foot.

Now that your lower body is in place just as in the sitting dive, stretch your hands above your head with the head tucked firmly between them. Bend your upper body so that the angle between your upper body and the left knee is reduced.

Take a deep breath and start lifting your hips and knees, keeping the movement of the upper body minimal and towards the water. Start sliding the right foot forward, towards the left foot, then take a slight spring with your left foot and straighten both legs out behind you (the push should be slightly upwards and forwards). The hands and upper body enter the water at an angle. When taking the push do not lift the upper body otherwise entry would be flat and painful.

Initially you may not be able to keep your legs straight and joined behind you or sometimes the entry may be too steep so your legs may flip over but you will learn with practise. Try to always enter at 45° angle.

Once you enter the water take a gradual glide and surface before you start a stroke or tread water.

Points to be Noted

1 The body should be relaxed.
2 Left foot should be at the pool edge and the right knee just next to it.

3 Head should be tucked between the hands and the body should be bent slightly forward.

4 Before the dive, after getting into position take a deep breath. This would also help you surface faster.

5 Push should be taken with your left foot slightly upward and forward.

6 After the entry, the glide should be shallow and hands should remain stretched with the head tucked between them, so as not to hit it against the pool floor.

7 This dive should be in at least six feet deep water to cater to error margins.

Plunge Dive

Stand on the starting block with your hands touching the side wall. Your feet should be slightly apart with the knees bent slightly. The eyes should be focused on the point of entry. Lift both hands upwards and let the body fall forward. Lift the heels. Take a deep breath and start swinging

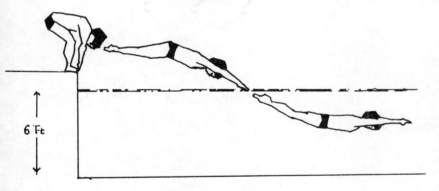

6 Ft

the hands downwards and forwards. The head comes up and is tucked between the arms. The legs straighten out, giving more push to the body. The body is to be absolutely straight and stretched at entry. The fingers enter the water first followed by hands, head, upper body and then the legs. The body is rigid until the feet have entered water. The entry of the body into the water should be at an angle of about 10° to 15°. The glide should be shallow and the same body momentum should be used to start your first stroke.

Points to Remember

1 Body should enter water at a 10° to 15° angle.
2 The body should be rigid and streamlined until it is fully submerged.
3 Glide should be shallow in the water.

WATER GAMES FOR FUN

Swimming in itself is a delightful sport, but while in the water specially for recreational purposes there are many water games which make it more interesting and fun.

Here are a few games which could make your stay in the water more interesting.

1. Treasure Hunt

Requirements—One Rupee Coin.

A person has to be selected to play the role of a king or queen who has the coin with him/her. The selected person then lines up all the subjects facing the wall of the pool side. Once everyone is lined up and facing the wall the king/queen then moves away to go and hide the treasure in the pool. Once that is done the king/queen moves away from that spot and comes out of the pool and asks her subjects to find the treasure hidden by him/her to make it easier clues can be given. The subject who finds the treasure then becomes the king/queen and the game goes on.

2. Blow the Ball

This is also a game wherein one can practise breathing and wading at the same time. This game can also be played during the initial periods of training.

Players line up at one end of the width in the shallow end. Each one has a table tennis ball placed in front of them. At a given command the race begins the players have to blow the ball across the width of the pool. The player whose ball touches the other wall first is the winner.

Another interesting game is the wading race in the shallow end. Players line up at one end of the width and place both hands behind their back or fold them in front of them and then race to the other end of the wall. It is more fun when players try to prevent each other from reaching the far end.

3. Swim—Between—Legs

Another common game is swimmers standing with their legs spread apart and one of them goes under water and swims between their legs and once he or she has crossed the last person they stand up and spread their legs to continue the chain and the first person in the chain starts the swim, and this continues.

4. Water Football

This is an excellent game to play in the shallow end of the

pool. The minimum members required are four a side. A plastic ball that float should be used. Goals are marked at both the widths of the shallow ends and the players line up in the middle of the pool. The ball is thrown between them and the players try and score goals using their feet to hit the ball. This is an excellent game for wading and balancing in water. And this game does not have goalkeepers—you could add your own rules for more fun.